This Is Me

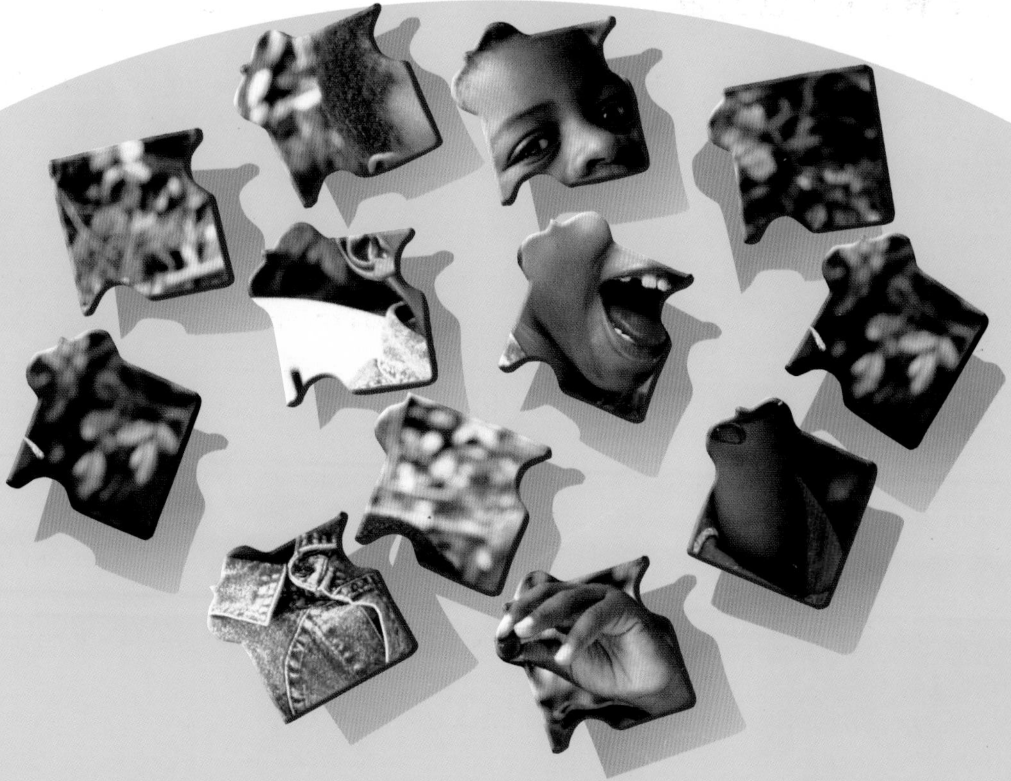

Chantelle Greenhills

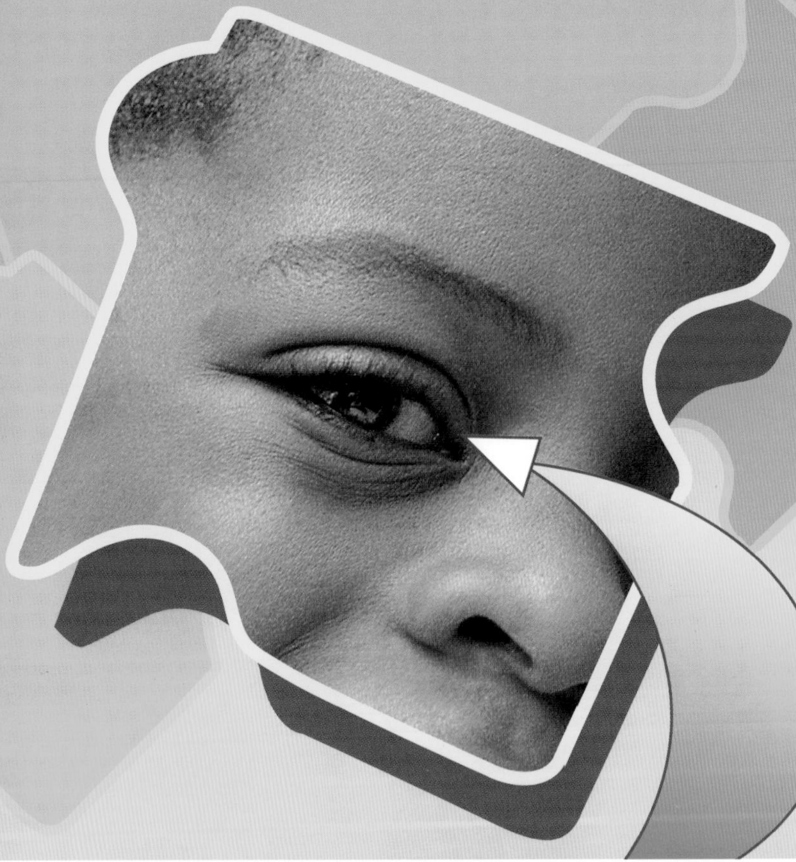

This is my eye.

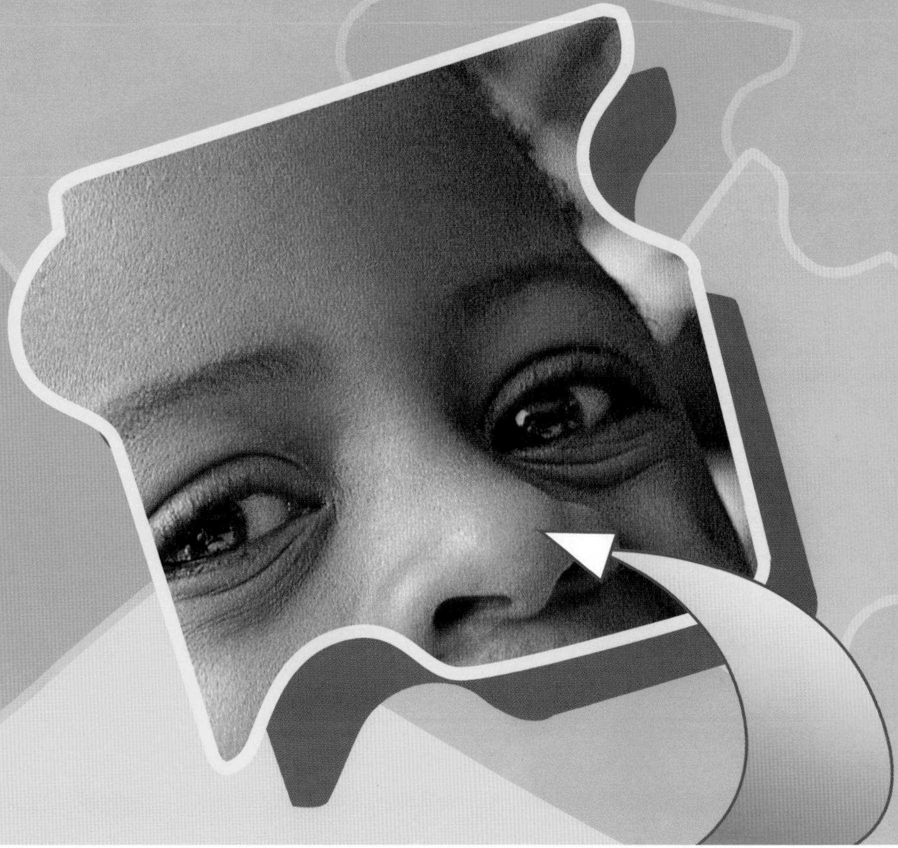

This is my nose.

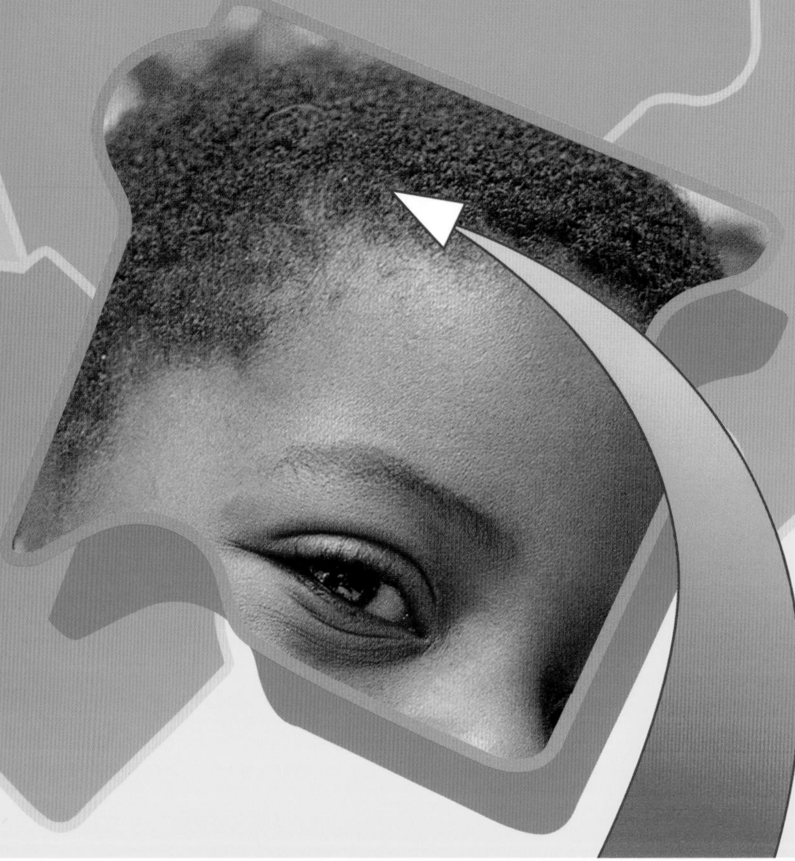

This is my hair.

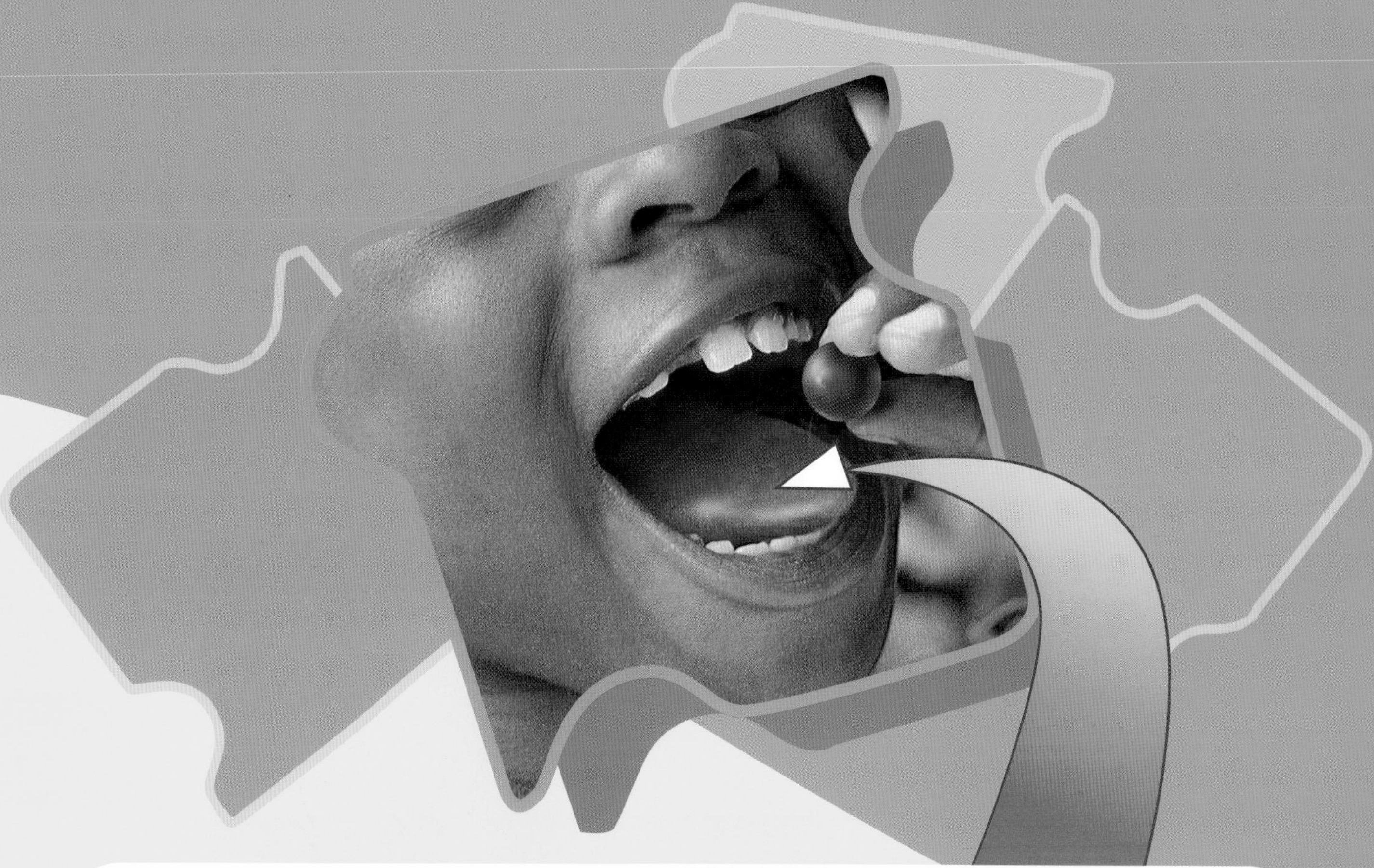

This is my tongue.

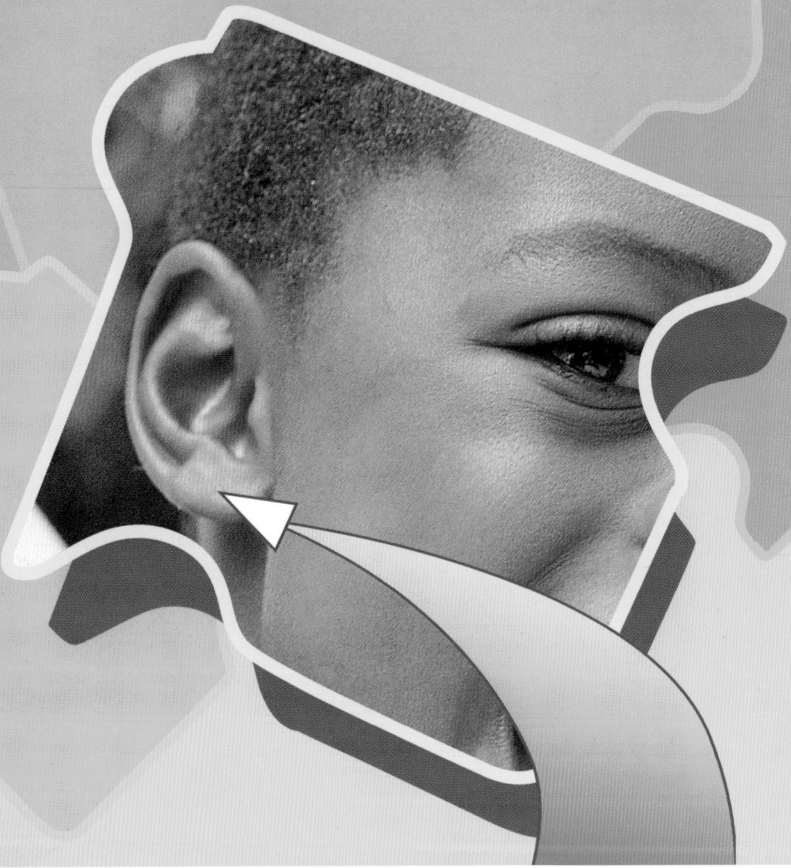

This is my ear.

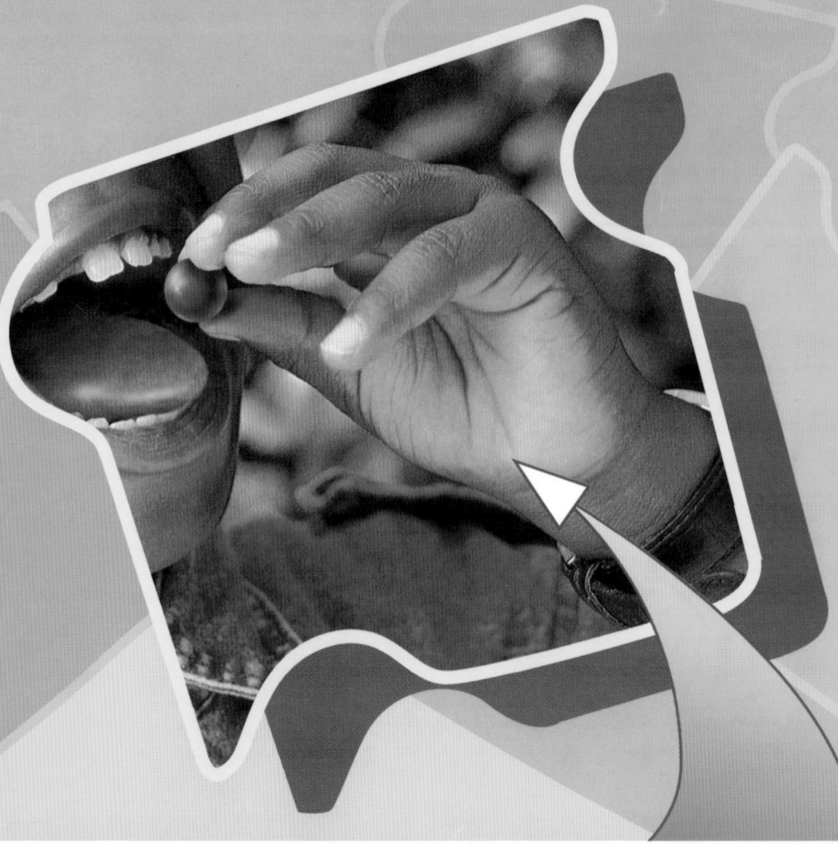

This is my hand.

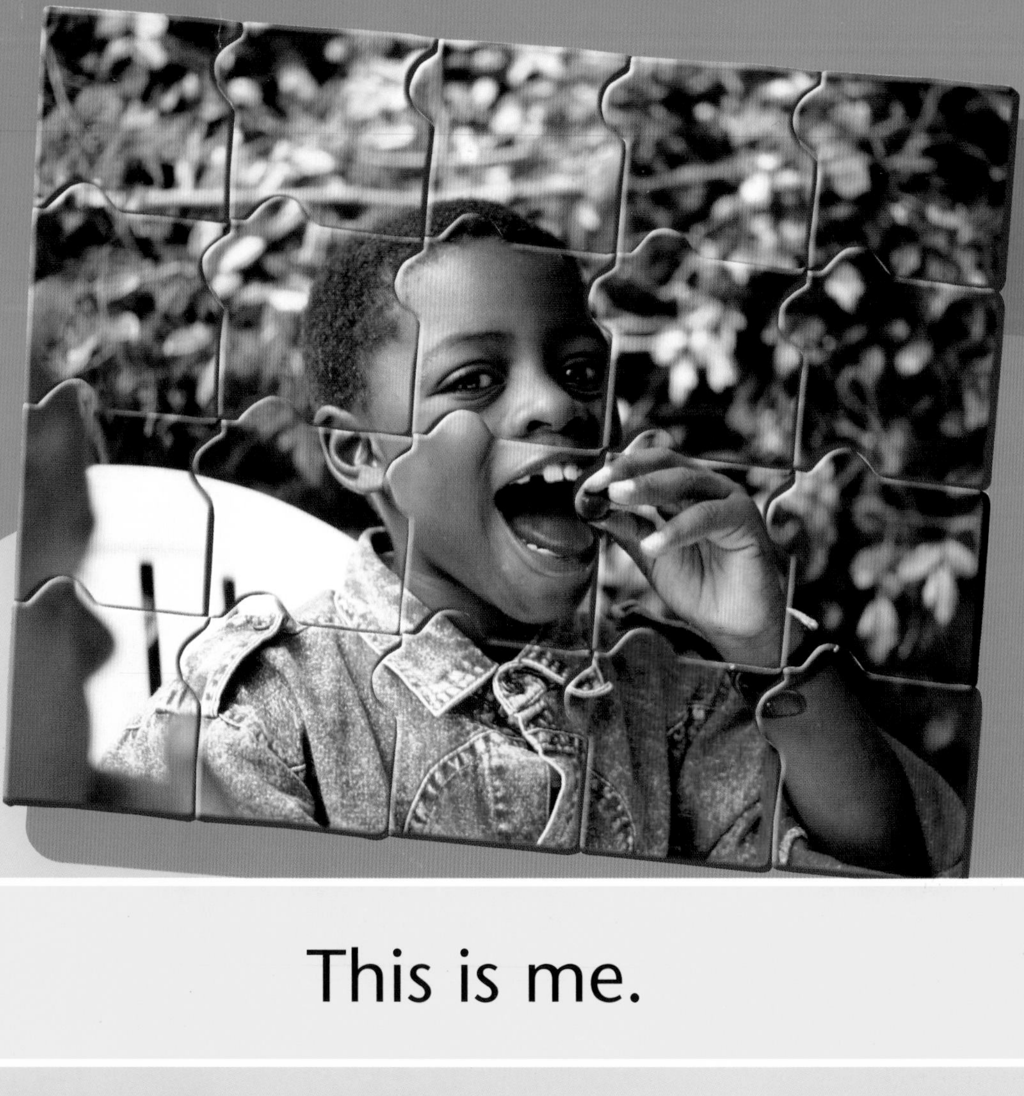

This is me.